Life in
Victorian Britain

The Victorians
at School

Rosemary Rees

Heinemann

First published in Great Britain by Heinemann Library
an imprint of Heinemann Publishers (Oxford) Ltd
Halley Court, Jordan Hill, Oxford OX2 8EJ

MADRID ATHENS PARIS FLORENCE PRAGUE WARSAW PORTSMOUTH NH CHICAGO
SAO PAULO SINGAPORE TOKYO MELBOURNE AUCKLAND IBADAN GABORONE JOHANNESBURG

© Rosemary Rees 1995

Designed by Ron Kamen, Green Door Design Ltd, Basingstoke, Hampshire
Colour Repro by Track QSP Ltd, London
Printed in Spain by Mateu Cromo Artes Graficas SA

99 98 97 96 95
10 9 8 7 6 5 4 3 2 1

ISBN 0 431 06668 X [HB]

99 98 97 96 95
10 9 8 7 6 5 4 3 2 1

ISBN 0 431 06682 5 [PB]

British Library Cataloguing in Publication Data
Rees, Rosemary
  Victorians at School. - (Life in Victorian Britain Series)
  I. Title II. Series
  941.081

Acknowledgements
The Publishers would like to thank the following for permission to reproduce photographs:
Barnaby's Picture Library: p. 15B
The Bridgeman Art Library: p. 22A
The Christopher Wood Gallery: p. 10A
A.C. Cooper Ltd: p. 8A
E.T. Archive: p. 13B
P.A. Gudgeon, p. 26A
Hulton Deutsch: p. 6A, p. 7B, 19A
The Illustrated London News Picture Library: p. 17D, p. 20A
J. Allan Cash Ltd: p. 4A
The Mansell Collection: p. 14A, p. 24A
The Mary Evans Picture Library: p. 21B, p. 23B, p. 27B, p. 29B

Cover photograph © Oxfordshire Photographic Archive, Centre for Oxfordshire Studies

Our thanks to Professor Eric Evans of the University of Lancaster for his comments in the preparation of this book.

Weights, measures and money

Victorians used a system of weights and measures that is not the same as the metric system we use now. The system the Victorians used is called the 'Imperial' system.

Imperial measures

Length
1 inch [2.5 cm]
12 inches (1 foot) [30.0 cm]
3 feet (1 yard) [1.0 m]
1,760 yards [1.6 km]

Capacity
1 pint [0.56 litres]
8 pints (1 gallon) [4.50 litres]

Weight
1 ounce (oz) [28 grams]
16 oz (1 pound 'lb') [.45 kg]
14 lbs (1 stone) [6.3 kg]
28 lbs (1 quarter) [12.75 kg]
4 qtrs (1 hundredweight 'cwt')
  [50.00 kg]
20 cwts (1 ton) [1 tonne]

Area
1 acre [0.40 hectares]

Money
4 farthings = 1 penny (1*d*)
2 halfpennies = 1 penny (1*d*)
12 pennies = 1 shilling
  (1/- or 1*s*)
20 shillings = £1

Contents

1 What did Victorian schools look like?

This is a modern photograph of a Victorian school. The school is in Walsall, in the West Midlands.

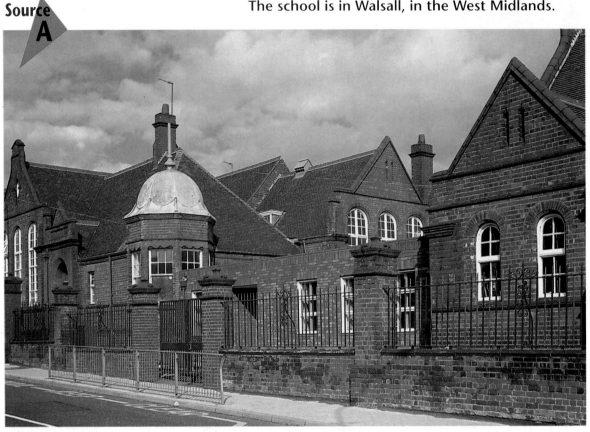

A lot of schools built in Victorian times are still used as schools today. Perhaps there is one near you. Most of these schools have been **modernized**. But if you look carefully you can see what they were like when Victorian children went to them. There were separate entrances for girls and boys. Teachers did not want boys and girls to mix too much once they were no longer in the Infants. The toilets were in a block outside in the playground. Sometimes the toilets were built years after the school building. When school toilets were first built they were not always connected to the **sewers**.

There were not always sewers to which they could be connected. The toilets were built in a separate block so that they could be emptied easily.

The ceilings in Victorian classrooms were very high. The windows were often too high up for children to look out of them. Teachers were afraid that the children would spend too long watching what was going on outside and would not pay attention to their lessons. Some schools had a school bell hanging in a little tower on the school roof. Teachers rang the bell when it was time for lessons to start and at the end of the school day.

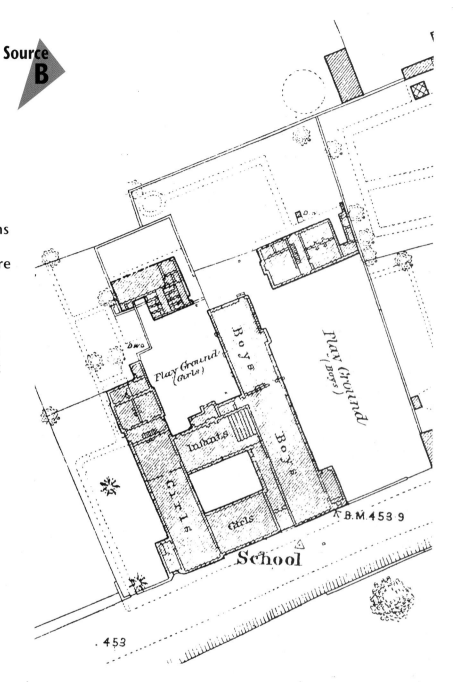

This is a plan of the **National school** in Tring, Hertfordshire. It was drawn in 1879. If you look carefully, you can see that the boys' playground is bigger than the girls' playground. The boys have bigger classrooms than the girls. This might be because there were more boys than girls in Tring at that time. It is much more likely, however, that it was because Victorian planners thought that boys needed more space than girls.

Source B

Play Ground (Girls)

Boys

Play Ground (Boys)

two

Infants

Boys

Girls

Girls

School

B.M. 453·9

·453

Source C

The school I go to was built in 1872. It has modern classrooms built on to it. There are two big old Victorian classrooms. There is a partition between them that the teachers fold back. This makes one big room where we have assembly and gym. We can't see out of the windows because they are too high up. The toilets are in the playground. They have heaters in them to keep them warm in the winter. My mum says that when she went to school the water in the toilets used to freeze in the winter.

David Vickery describes the primary school he goes to in a village outside Cambridge.

5

2 Rich children: public schools and governesses

Girls and boys whose parents were rich did not always go to school. When they were six, seven and eight years old girls and boys had lessons together. They had lessons at home. They were taught to read and write by a woman called a **governess**. When they could read and write properly, and knew a little history and geography, everything changed.

Boys

Some boys stayed at home but they were not taught by a governess any more. They were taught by a man called a **tutor**. The boys learned Greek and Latin, mathematics and French. Usually the boys were sent away to school. They went to **public schools** like Eton, Rugby or Charterhouse.

These were **boarding schools**. In these schools the boys learned much the same as they would have learned from a tutor. They played a lot of sport as well. This was supposed to teach them how to work together as a team. However, many boys were teased and **bullied** by the masters and by older boys.

Victorians thought that this sort of education would make sure the boys grew up as young gentlemen who would know how to behave in upper-class society. They thought the boys would be able to look after their **estates**, become **Members of Parliament** or become officers in the British army when they grew up. In these ways they would serve their country.

Source A

This picture of a classroom in Eton College was drawn in 1861.

Girls

Rich Victorian parents wanted their daughters to make good marriages with wealthy young men. This meant that they had to learn certain things. They had to learn how to keep household accounts and deal with servants. These they learned from their mother. Rich girls had to be able to sing and play the piano; they had to be able to paint, dance and do **embroidery**. They learned these things from a governess. Sometimes a girl's parents would hire a drawing master or a dancing master who would give them some lessons every week. Sometimes, if they had sons too, the boys' tutor would give his sisters some French conversation lessons. In all these ways, rich Victorians hoped to turn their daughters into suitable wives and mothers.

This photograph of young ladies with their tutor was taken in 1851. It is called *The Geography Lesson.*

3 Middle-class children: grammar schools and academies

There were many different kinds of schools to which middle-class parents sent their children.

Boys

Some boys went to local **grammar schools**. There the boys learned the sorts of subjects that would be useful to them when they became businessmen, tradesmen or managers in industry. They learned writing, arithmetic, geography, mathematics and French. If a boy went to one of the older grammar schools, he learned Latin and Greek as well.

Some boys went to **proprietary schools**. These schools were set up by local businessmen in **industrial** towns. The boys learned things like **book-keeping** and arithmetic, French and geography. These would be useful when they went to work in local businesses.

Source B

There are in all parts of the School many boys with knowledge of Geography, English Grammar, and History and Arithmetic. Many of the younger boys have been carefully grounded in Latin and French grammar. In the Senior School there has been much reading of Latin. As to Mathematics, the work has been for most boys only a preparation, but there are boys reading subjects like Trigonometry, Conic Sections and Analytic Geometry.

Mr Keeling was the Headmaster of Bradford Grammar School between 1872 and 1916. This is part of what he wrote about the school in 1872.

A picture of Battle School in Sussex, which was built in 1847. A building looking solid and serious, like this one, was supposed to impress parents. They were supposed to think that their sons would be taught well if they were sent there.

Source A

Hopewell House, North Road

Horsforth, near Leeds

Mrs Hartley's School for Young Ladies

Terms per Quarter

For Tuition in all Branches of an English Education

Boarders above 12 year of age	£6. 0. 0
Boarders under 12 years of age	£5. 0. 0
Day pupils above 12 years of age	£1. 1. 0
Day pupils under 12 years of age	£0. 15. 0
Music	£1. 0. 0
French	£1. 1. 0
Drawing	£0. 10. 6
Laundress	£0. 10. 0

Each young lady to come with Slippers, Pillow cases, Towels, Toilet soap, Fork and Spoon

This is an advertisement for a girls' school near Leeds. There were lots of academies like this in Victorian times before 1870.

Girls

Girls from middle-class families went to school if their parents wanted them to. Many doctors, managers and shopkeepers couldn't afford **governesses**, but they wanted their daughters to learn. People set up **academies**. Here girls were taught subjects like drawing and music, arithmetic and French. Some schools were good and some were very bad. One girls' school that was very good was the North London Collegiate School. This was opened in London by Frances Mary Buss in 1850.

There were not many schools like it in Victorian times. Here girls learned all the subjects their brothers were learning at grammar schools and proprietary schools. Parents and teachers expected girls from schools like this to go on to be more than just wives and mothers when they grew up. Some of them were the first women to go to university. They became the first women doctors and lawyers. Others became explorers and painters.

4 Poor children: dame schools and common day-schools

This picture of a village dame school was painted by Alfred Rankley in 1855. The school seems to be in the dame's front room. She is teaching the alphabet to one child. Others are looking at pictures on a screen. Can you see anybody being naughty?

In 1880 **Parliament** said that every boy and girl under ten years old had to go to school. Before 1880 many children from poor families did not go to school at all. The schools were not free. Some of the children's parents worked in mines, factories and fields. Some parents didn't have any work at all. They couldn't pay the school teacher to teach their children. Being forced to send their children to school caused great hardship. Poor families needed every penny the children could earn. They couldn't let their children have time away from work to go to school.

Dame schools

Many working-class children who did go to school went to **dame schools**. These schools were run by elderly women who wanted to make a bit of money. They charged about fourpence a week for each pupil. Some of the 'dames' did their best to teach reading and some writing. Some of them were really only child-minders.

Common day-schools

Most children stayed at dame schools until they were six or seven years old. Then they went to work. However, if their parents could afford to pay about ninepence a week, children could go on to **common day-schools**. These schools taught the children reading, writing and arithmetic as well as some history and geography. This sort of education meant that the children could go on to get jobs as, for example, shop assistants and clerks.

Workshop schools

Almost anyone could set up a school. Shoe-makers, tailors, blacksmiths and carpenters sometimes set up small schools in their workshops. They taught reading and writing and something about their own trade.

Source C

Our fee was a penny a week. Our dame had her own way of controlling us by means of a leather lash tied to a stout walking stick. We often tried to get near the door and while the teacher dozed we slipped into the fields and lanes and into the sunshine.

John Sykes remembers what his dame school was like.

Workshop schools were important. Many of them taught the children of skilled workers how important it was to be able to read and write and argue properly. Some of these children organized and ran **trades unions** when they were adults.

Source B

There were, in our family, ten children, that is six boys called Frederick, George, Harry, Edwin, Sydney and Herbert Charles, and four girls, Mary-Ann, Jane, Emma and Fanny.

When I was three I was sent to a Dame's School, kept for very young children by a person named Whitehead. I remember the teacher giving me a needle and thread and piece of rag to pass away my time during one afternoon.

I was next sent to another Dame's School, kept by Ma'am Lund. If a boy was naughty he was shut in her dark pantry as a punishment. One culprit ate up some cold plum pudding that was in the pantry. I do not remember what punishment he had for this, but the pantry was not used for this purpose for some time after.

Sometimes I was taken out for a walk on a Sunday, and if we went near this school I remember I used to run as fast as possible in case I was taken in to it. So it seems I did not like it very much.

Frederick Hobley was born at Thame, Oxfordshire, in 1833. He went to a dame school, a National school and then trained to be a teacher. He stayed a teacher until 1871 . Then he worked as a commercial traveller and a book-keeper. He retired in 1899. Six years later, his children persuaded him to write about his life. This is part of what he wrote about his time at the dame schools.

5 Poor children: Sunday schools

What was Sunday school?

Sunday schools were started long before Queen Victoria came to the throne in 1837. At the end of the eighteenth century a man called Robert Raikes saw children playing in the streets. They were filthy, dressed in rags and swearing loudly. It was a Sunday. Robert Raikes decided that there were better things the children could be doing. He thought the children should be in school. The problem was that the children were at work during the week. So Robert Raikes decided to start schools that only opened on Sundays. In 1780 he opened four Sunday schools in Gloucester. This was the beginning of the Sunday School Movement.

Who went?

By 1851 there were about 23,000 Sunday schools in Britain. Over two million children went to them for two or three hours on Sundays. Not all the children went every Sunday. Girls and boys learned stories from the Bible. Some learned how to read. By the end of Queen Victoria's reign in 1901, nearly six million children were going to Sunday schools.

Where did the money come from?

Important people in the towns thought that Sunday schools were a good idea. This was because Sunday schools kept the children off the streets. It was also because the children learned to read the Bible and were taught how to behave by being told stories about men and women who were good. Some factory owners forced the children who worked for them to go to school on Sundays.

The well-off people in towns gave money to pay the Sunday school teachers. They gave money to buy books, **slates** and other equipment. They thought that children and young people who attended would behave well, work well and would not make trouble. Others thought that poor children should not be taught to read and write. They were afraid the poor would begin having dangerous ideas: they might begin asking whether it was right that some people were so rich whilst others were so poor.

Source A

Sundays were hateful days. My mother sent us to the Primitive Methodist because school began earlier and we had longer sessions and she wanted to get rid of us for as long as possible. What we learned there for my own good I have no idea. The children behaved very badly. Teachers were a queer, mixed crowd who knew little about what they were supposed to teach. They gave us to understand that we were in danger of hell fire if we were not good. I knew there was no hope whatever for me.

Faith Osgerby wrote her autobiography, *My Memoirs*, at the end of the nineteenth century. This is part of what she wrote about going to Sunday school.

Source
C

I was made to learn by heart long passages of Scripture. I did not understand them, or even try to do so. As to the hymns which I learned, and repeated to my teachers, I am amazed that books containing them were ever put into the hands of children. Of course, like everybody in the school, I learned:

There is a dreadful hell
And everlasting pains
Where sinners must with devils dwell
In darkness, fire and chains.

Hell was a very real thing to me.

Marianne Farningham wrote a book in 1900 called *A Working Woman's Life*. This is part of what she wrote about the time she went to Sunday school. Marianne was born in Farningham, Kent, in 1833. Her father was Joseph Hearn who was a tradesman.

This photograph of children outside their Sunday school was taken in 1896.

6 Poor children: ragged schools

This picture is called *A New Pupil for John Pounds*. It was painted by E. H. Wehnert and shows what the artist thought the first ragged school looked like.

Ragged schools were for the very poorest children. They were started almost by accident. A cobbler called John Pounds lived and worked in Portsmouth. He worried about the gangs of hungry, filthy children who roamed the streets. He let them come in to his workshop to get warm. From about 1818 he taught them some reading and writing and a little about shoe-making and shoe-mending. The school was free: John Pounds did not charge parents anything. John Pounds hoped that by doing this he would help them to find a job.

Money for ragged schools

Some important, well-off people thought John Pounds' idea was a good one. They set up charities to run ragged schools in the towns where they lived. By 1844, when there were about a hundred ragged schools in Britain, a Ragged School Union was set up.

The aim of the Union was to let everyone know about the good work ragged schools were doing, and to raise money to start new ones. Lord Shaftesbury, who was the chairman of the Union, even begged money from **Members of Parliament** as they went in and out of the **House of Commons**. Within 25 years the number of ragged schools in Britain had doubled to 200.

Some people thought that ragged schools did more harm than good. They thought that if very poor people were taught to read and write, it would just make them better thieves, pickpockets and robbers. They would then, at the very least, know the value of what they were stealing. They could sell the goods for the best price.

Source B

Source C

At the ragged school I learned reading, writing, tailoring, shoe-making and cleaning the place. There were forty or fifty boys. Half of them were thieves. We would teach any good boys to thieve.

A young man who had gone to a ragged school when he was a boy told Henry Mayhew what it was like. Henry Mayhew wrote down what he said and printed it in his book, *London Labour and the London Poor*, which was published in 1851.

This drawing of Lambeth Ragged School was printed in *The Illustrated London News* in 1846.

7 Poor children: workhouse and factory schools

A few years before Victoria became Queen in 1837, **Parliament** passed two important Acts. These were partly to do with teaching two special groups of children to read and write.

Factory schools

The first group of children were those who worked in factories and **mills** that made cloth. In 1833 a Factory Act said that all children under the age of thirteen who were working in textile factories and mills had to go to school for two hours every week. The Act also said that there were to be special **inspectors**. These would make sure the children were working only the hours they should, and that they were being taught properly. In 1844 another Factory Act was passed by Parliament. This Act said that children aged between eight and thirteen who worked in factories had to spend three full or six half days a week in school.

Workhouse schools

The second group of children were those in **workhouses**. Families who were too poor to look after themselves often went into workhouses to live. There they got food and clothes. In 1834 Parliament passed an Act which laid down all sorts of rules and regulations to do with workhouses. Amongst other things, it said that there should be teachers for the children who lived in workhouses.

How good were these schools?

Some factory schools were good, but there were many that were not. Some classes were held in dusty boiler rooms or draughty engine sheds. The children were crowded in for two hours a days and did not learn very much at all. In some workhouses the 'teachers' were other inmates who could hardly read or write themselves.

Source A

The children have their toys and a small library. Boys and girls go out together for walks three times a week. The boys have their allotments which they can work on as they like. They play cricket in the workhouse fields. Both boys and girls go to Sunday school and they are often sent out on errands. The children were at play as we walked to the door, the boys at cricket and the girls with skipping ropes. Their voices sounded very merry.

In 1878 an inspector visited a workhouse school. Forty children went to the school. This is part of his report.

The private factory schools are on the whole unsatisfactory. In two, taught in cottage rooms by old, incapacitated weavers, hardly any of the children learn writing and none could do more in reading than scramble through an easy verse in the New Testament.

This is part of a report from an inspector who visited some factory schools in Rochdale, Lancashire, in 1861.

This picture of a government inspector with children in a factory school was drawn in 1881 and published in a magazine called *The Illustrated London News.*

The children seemed to read well, but on looking at their books I found that many were held upside down. The children could not read at all, but had been taught to repeat certain sentences and to hold their books in front of them as if they were reading.

This is part of a report made by an inspector who visited a workhouse in 1868.

Here the factory owners have provided a well warmed and well ventilated room, and they have employed a good master and mistress. Reading, writing and arithmetic are taught to the children and the girls are taught needlework.

Part of a report from an inspector who visited a factory school in Manchester in the 1860s.

8 Poor children: church schools

Some of the people who went to church on Sundays, and some of their priests and ministers, wanted children from poor families to go to school. Sunday schools only opened on Sundays and there were not very many **ragged schools**. They set up organizations that ran schools during the week for poor children. By the beginning of Queen Victoria's reign, the British and Foreign Schools Society was running over a hundred schools. The National Society for the Education of the Poor was running more than 400 schools. The government began giving money to these two Church societies in 1833. At the start this money was used to keep the school buildings in good condition.

The monitorial system

By 1837 most of the children in these British and **National schools** were taught by monitors. One teacher taught some facts to a small group of older children. These children, called monitors, told groups of younger children these facts and tested them. Then the monitors went back to the teacher to be told some more facts. The problem was that the younger children didn't really learn properly. Mostly, they only repeated back to the monitors what the monitors had just said to them.

Pupil teachers

In 1839 **Parliament** said that there were to be **inspectors** who went round these schools making sure the government's money was being spent properly. The man in charge was James Kay-Shuttleworth. He said that the monitors didn't really teach anything at all but were just there to control the children. He started a new system. One pupil was taught enough to teach the whole class properly. This pupil-teacher had extra training and eventually became a teacher.

Payment by results

In 1861 there were three and a half million children in Britain. Less than half of them went to school regularly. Only one in ten of the children who did go to school could read, write and do easy sums. In 1862, Robert Lowe, the minister in the government in charge of education, started something new. Children in a school were divided into six classes, called standards. Each standard was tested by inspectors. How much a teacher was paid depended on how well that teacher's pupils had learned during the year.

Lots of teachers just taught their pupils what they knew the inspector was going to test. For example, teachers were told which reading book the inspector was going to ask the children to read. Many children spent the whole year practising reading that one book over and over again. In 1864 58,000 children passed standards 4 to 6. By 1870 the number was 96,000. This system was called 'Payment by results'.

A school with a teacher and monitors, drawn in 1839. The teacher is sitting behind a desk at the front of the class. The monitors are standing by groups of younger pupils they are supposed to be teaching. The kites and other toys hanging from the ceiling were given to the pupils who have done good work, for them to play with.

Source B

A Lesson on a cup

Monitor:	What is a cup made of?
Pupils:	Gold, silver, china.
Monitor:	Who drinks out of gold cups?
Pupils:	The king.
Monitor:	Who drinks out of china cups?
Pupils:	Poor people.
Monitor:	What is the inside of a cup?
Pupils:	Hollow.

This is part of a lesson about a cup which monitors taught to younger pupils. It is from a text book written in 1837

Source C

Two inspectors came once a year and carried out a dramatic inspection. The school master came into the school in his best suit; all the pupils and pupil-teachers would be listening until at ten o'clock a dog-cart would be heard on the road even though it was eighty yards away. In would come two gentlemen looking very important and with deep, rich voices. Each would sit at a desk and children would be called in turn to one or the other. The master hovered round, calling out children as they were needed. The children would see him start with vexation [crossness] as a good pupil stuck on a word in the reading book he had been reading all year, or sat without moving with his sum in front of him. The master's anxiety was deep, for his earnings depended on the children's work.

Joseph Ashby went to school in the 1860s. When he was an old man he told his daughter what it had been like. She wrote it all down, as well as other things about his life. The book she wrote about her father was published in 1961. It is called *Joseph Ashby of Tysoe*.

9 Poor children: board schools

In 1867 an Act of **Parliament** gave the vote to a lot of working-class men. This meant they could vote for **Members of Parliament**. In 1870 the government decided that something had to be done about education. Robert Lowe was the minister in charge of education. He said, in the **House of Commons**, that when the poor children who couldn't read or write became adults, they would be able to vote. It was therefore important that as many children as possible were educated. A government minister, William Forster, was given the job of seeing that this was done.

William Forster said that England should be divided into districts. Parliament agreed. Every district had to have enough good schools for young children. If there weren't enough, local **ratepayers** had to **elect** a group of people called a school board. Most of the new school boards were in towns. The school board had to set up new schools for children up to ten years old. These schools were paid for partly by the government and partly from the local rates. At first, parents had to pay a few pence to send their children to board schools. Then in 1891 board schools were made free.

Source A

This picture shows school board officers in London. They are rounding up children who should be in school. The drawing was published in *The Illustrated London News* in 1871.

This photograph of an assembly at a board school was taken in 1900.

Every morning at 9 o'clock we were rung into the schoolroom by a bell on the roof. We sang the morning hymn (*Awake My Soul*) led by a **harmonium** which one of the monitors played. I do not remember ever singing another opening hymn. None of us knew the right wording. A prayer by the master followed and then he mounted his platform desk and filled up the register while we were given a lesson from the Old Testament by a monitor. Now and then the monitor stopped and questioned us; those whose answers were wrong were called from their seats to stand in line in the front. When the scripture lesson was over the master caned all the boys, and now and then a girl, who were standing out in the line.

Walter Rose was a carpenter's son. He went to a board school. When he was much older he wrote about his time there. This is what he wrote about assemblies.

10 Board schools: lessons

In 1901, at the end of Queen Victoria's reign, all children had to go to school until they were thirteen years old. If they went to board schools, their parents did not have to pay anything at all.

Many new schools were built. Up until then, children had been divided into 'standards', all working in the same room. Now the 'standards' had their own classrooms and their own teacher. They sat on wooden benches and worked at wooden desks. Many wrote on **slates** which could be wiped clean. Some children had exercise books in which to write, and older children had text books and library books.

What did they teach?

Many teachers taught far more than just the subjects that were going to be tested by the **inspectors**. Children learned history, geography and drawing. The boys did woodwork and the girls did domestic science. Some children even did scientific experiments. All children had PE lessons in the playground. For some this meant running and jumping and playing ball games. For most children it meant marching round and round and doing arm swinging exercises. All children learned to read and write, even though some of them weren't very good at it.

Source A

This is a page from an alphabet book of old rhymes. Children learned to read from books like this.

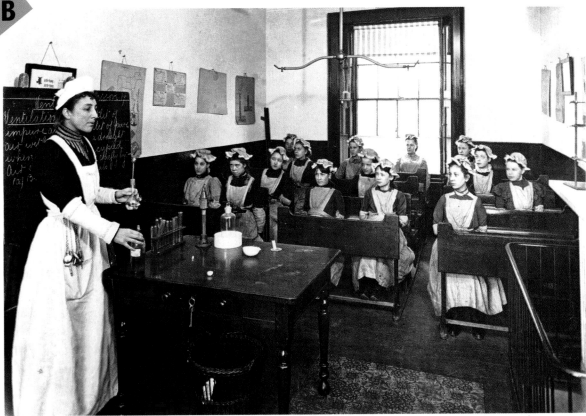

Arithmetic was considered the most important of the subjects taught. The writing lesson consisted of the copying of copperplate sayings: 'A fool and his money are soon parted', 'Waste not, want not' and so on. Once a week composition would be set, usually in the form of writing a letter describing some recent event. History readers were in use containing such stories as Alfred and the cakes. No geography was taught. But on the walls of the classroom were hung splendid maps. Once a day a class would be called out for a reading lesson. Her Majesty's Inspector of Schools came once a year.

Flora Thompson went to a board school. Years later she wrote about what life was like when she was a child, in a book called *Lark Rise to Candleford*. It was published in 1945.

This photograph of girls at a board school was taken in 1900. They are being taught all sorts of things they need to know about running a house and being a housewife. Here they are learning about ventilation.

Who was Henry VIII?

The son of Henry VII.

What was his character?

As a young man he was bluff, generous, right royal and handsome.

How was he when he grew older?

He was bloated, vain, cruel and selfish.

This is from a history text book called *My First Book of the History of England*, which was published in 1864. It was used for many years in board schools.

11 Board schools: playtime and punishments

Playtime

In Victorian times children did not have long playtimes. School was for work and learning. But children did play games in the playground before school began, and when they were allowed out at lunch-time.

On the plan of a school on page 5 you will see that the boys had a bigger playground than the girls. This was because the Victorians expected boys to play rougher games than girls. They played football and cricket; they played 'tig' and marbles. Sometimes they fought each other.

Victorians did not expect girls to need as much space as boys for the games they played. Girls played skipping and counting games; they played hopscotch and 'let's pretend' games.

This print of girls playing a skipping game was made in 1885.

Punishment

In Victorian times children were often punished when they were at school. They were punished when they were naughty. They were punished when they didn't learn something properly. They were punished when they forgot what they had learned. Often the punishment was being hit, by the teacher or by monitors, with a stick. Many children were afraid of school because of this. Many children couldn't learn properly because they were afraid of being hit. Some children learned properly to avoid being hit.

Source A

B

She was ugly: she couldn't help her ancient, sallow, wrinkled skin, which hung under her neck and chin in disgusting folds, or the yellow-tinted whites of her eyes, but she could help being cruel and unloving. The only words I ever heard her speak were harsh, bad-tempered ones. It was the big girls of the school she vented her **sadistic** instincts on, and she would bring down her beastly cane on the palms, one on each hand, with such a full-arm action and sickening thwack that I was terrified that the hand would drop off at the wrist.

Daisy Cowper remembered her head teacher when she was at school in Liverpool in the 1890s. This is part of what she wrote about her.

Source

C

The main idea was to get us out to earn money. The schooling was based on discipline. Reading, writing and arithmetic were essential, and children were clobbered until they mastered them. We were severely caned (with a stick) unless too bad an offence had been committed – then the Head had a special session on our behinds with the thonged leather. At least, we knew where we stood – we certainly couldn't sit!

Nowadays children are not caned or beaten when they are at school. Hitting children was very common in Victorian times. They believed it was the only way to make children behave and learn. Beating children in school did not end at the end of Queen Victoria's reign. Jim Tait was born in 1899. Here he remembers the beatings at school when he was a boy at the beginning of the twentieth century.

Source

D

He tanned them and whacked their backs – we thought he was never going to stop. Whack! Whack! The skin was broke! We stared in silence, never said a word – we daren't.

Next morning we heard a cufuffle in the entrance. The two mothers had arrived. They said they'd smash him up. They'd have given him summat if they could have copped him, but he escaped out the back door.

George Hewins went to school in Stratford-upon-Avon in Warwickshire. He watched while his teacher beat two boys. This is part of what he wrote about what happened. It was published in 1981 in a book called *The Dillen*.

Source

E

In winter, at dinner-time, those children who came from a distance were allowed to sit round the stove to eat their food, but afterwards had to go out-of-doors for the rest of the hour. No milk was provided and no food was available. Everything had to be brought from home. After dinner the children had to amuse themselves as best they could in their own way. The playground was small, and the pupils were forced out on the roads for most of their games. No one thought it worthwhile to provide a proper playing field for the children.

Charles Cooper was born in 1872. When he was a boy he lived and went to school in Walton, a mining village near Wakefield in West Yorkshire. When he was 92 he wrote down what he remembered about his life. This is part of what he wrote about dinner-times and playtimes when he was at school.

12 Adults at school

In 1876 **Parliament** decided that all children had to go to school until they were ten years old. Before 1876 there were many thousands of children who never went to school or who only went to school for a very short time. Most of these children were from working-class families. Whether or not they went to school depended on whether there was a school within walking distance of their home. It also depended on whether their parents could afford to pay the school fee, and whether there were jobs for children in the area. Very often poor families depended on the few pence the children could earn. All this meant that there were thousands of adults who were clever but who had never learned to read or write when they were children.

After a hard day's work, many of these adults struggled to learn to read and write and to learn about things like history and politics. Some of them taught themselves. Farmworkers went off into the fields and woods on Sundays; factory workers struggled to learn to read in attic bedrooms by candlelight. Sometimes groups of friends helped each other to learn to read and write with whatever books they could get hold of. In large towns there was often a **Mechanics' Institute**. There, teachers ran evening classes for men wanting to become engineers and mechanics. Mechanics' Institutes also had libraries and many working men joined these Institutes just so that they could use the library. Many adults just wanted to learn. This was important in Victorian times.

Source A

This is a modern photograph of a Victorian Mechanics' Institute.
This Mechanics' Institute is in Bacup, Lancashire.

This picture of working men from Louth, Lincolnshire, at an evening class was drawn in 1855.

Many of these working men became interested in poetry and the books of famous writers; some wrote their own poetry. Some stayed in their old jobs and joined **trades unions**, pushing for better pay and conditions for working people. Others went on to better jobs and some of them wrote their **autobiographies**. They gave them titles like *Workman's Cottage to Windsor Castle* and *From Chimney-boy to Councillor*. Very, very few women learned in this way when they were adults. This was mainly because most Victorians, especially in the first part of the nineteenth century, believed that education was something for boys and men, not girls and women.

Source
C

I felt a sudden, strange sense of wretchedness. There was a blighting consciousness that my lot was harsher than his and that of others. I went back to my mould-running and hot stove with my first anguish in my heart.

Charles Tunstall was born in Tunstall in 1832. In 1840, when he was eight years old, he was working in a big pottery. He saw a young man sitting reading a book. Many years later he described what he felt when he wrote about his life in his book, *When I was a Child, by an Old Potter*. The book was published in 1903.

13 Schools in Victorian stories

Victorian authors like Charles Dickens and Charlotte Brontë wrote about boys' and girls' school days in their stories. Of course they may have made things seem especially bad or especially good just to make the story interesting. However, they cannot have been far away from the truth otherwise their readers would not have bought their books. So what they have to say tells us something about schools in Victorian times. It also tells us what the authors wanted us to believe about schools in Victorian times.

This picture is from one of Charles Dickens books, *Nicholas Nickleby*, which was published in 1838. The story is about Nicholas Nickleby who was a teacher at 'Dotheboys Hall', which was run by a Mr Squeers. In this picture the boys are being dosed with treacle and brimstone. The boys were very badly treated and hardly learned anything at all. 'Dotheboys Hall' was based on what Charles Dickens knew about a real school in Yorkshire. Some of the people who read the book were so angry about the ways in which the boys were treated in the story that they did all they could to make sure that real schools treated their children properly.

I want to be A1 at cricket and football and all the other games. I want to get into the Sixth [a class] and please the Doctor [Dr Arnold, the head teacher] and I want to carry away just as much Latin and Greek as will take me through Oxford University respectably and I want to leave behind me the name of a fellow who never bullied a little boy or turned his back on a big one.

Thomas Hughes was a pupil at Rugby School when a man called Dr Arnold was the head teacher there. When he grew up, Thomas Hughes wrote a book called *Tom Brown's Schooldays* which was published in 1857. It was about a boy called Tom Brown who went to Rugby School. In this extract Tom is explaining what he wants to do while he is at the school.

A chapter having been read through twice, the books were closed and the girls examined. The lesson was about the reign of Charles I, and there were questions about tonnage, and poundage, and ship money, which most of them could not answer. Burns was ready with answers on every point. I kept expecting Miss Scatcherd to praise her, but she suddenly cried out, 'You dirty, disagreeable girl! You have never cleaned your nails this morning!' Burns made no answer. 'Why,' I thought, 'does she not explain that she could neither clean her nails nor wash her face as the water was frozen?' Burns unloosed her pinafore. The teacher instantly and sharply inflicted on her neck a dozen strokes with a bunch of twigs.

This comes from a story, *Jane Eyre*, which was written by Charlotte Brontë in 1847. In the story Jane was sent to Lowood Hall, a boarding school for orphan girls. Here Jane is describing what happened to a friend of hers, Helen Burns, during a history lesson.

This picture is from a Victorian story called *Tom Brown's Schooldays*, by Thomas Hughes. This shows a dormitory at Rugby School where the boys slept at night.

GLOSSARY

academy a boarding or day school for middle-class young ladies

autobiography the story of a person's life written by the person concerned

boarding school a school where the pupils attending would live at the school during term-time

book-keeping keeping accounts, which are records of money received and money spent

bullied a person who is bullied is made to do something by force and because they are afraid of the bully

charities organizations that help the poor and needy

cobbler a person who mends shoes

commercial travellers people who travel the country for a manufacturer, selling the manufacturer's goods to shops so that they can sell them on to their customers

common day-school a local school for working-class children from around the age of six, who had to pay to attend

dame schools schools runs by elderly women in their own homes

embroidery sewing pictures or patterns with coloured threads

elect vote for something or someone

estate land belonging to a rich person

governess an educated middle-class woman who was paid to live with a rich family to educate the daughters, and also the sons before they were old enough to have a male tutor

grammar school a local school where middle-class parents paid for their sons to be educated

harmonium a musical instrument which looks rather like a piano but which works by using bellows and metal reeds

House of Commons all the elected Members of Parliament, or the part of the building (Houses of Parliament) where the Members of Parliament meet

industrial connected with industry

inspectors people appointed by the government to inspect schools to make sure children were being taught properly and that the law was being obeyed

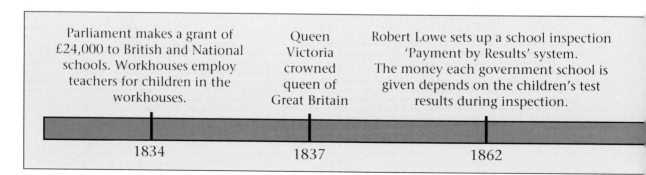

Parliament makes a grant of £24,000 to British and National schools. Workhouses employ teachers for children in the workhouses.

Queen Victoria crowned queen of Great Britain

Robert Lowe sets up a school inspection 'Payment by Results' system. The money each government school is given depends on the children's test results during inspection.

1834   1837   1862

Institute club or meeting place for members of a trade or profession

mechanic a skilled worker who makes, works or repairs machinery

Member of Parliament a person elected to the House of Commons to represent all the people living in a certain area called a constituency

mill type of factory where things such as cotton were made

modernize bring up to date

national school a school for poor children, run by the national Society for the Education of the Poor

Parliament the House of Commons and the House of Lords

proprietary school a local school for middle-class boys set up by businessmen in some industrial towns

public schools the most important and well-thought of boarding schools for boys

ragged school a free school for poor children, usually run with charity money

ratepayer a person who pays a set amount of money each year to their local council

sadistic taking pleasure out of being cruel

school board school boards were set up by the Education Act of 1870; they were groups of people who were chosen to run board schools

sewer a pipe taking waste away from a lavatory or sink

slate a thin plate of grey rock, about the size of an exercise book and usually in a wooden frame, on which children wrote

trades unions groups of workers who join together into an organization to push for better working conditions

tutor a middle-class man paid to live with a rich family and educate the sons

workhouse a place where the very poor went for food and shelter

workshop school a small school set up by a skilled worker in his workshop

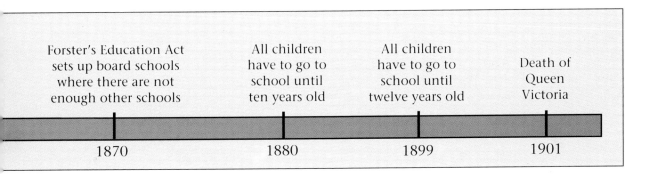

Forster's Education Act sets up board schools where there are not enough other schools	All children have to go to school until ten years old	All children have to go to school until twelve years old	Death of Queen Victoria
1870	1880	1899	1901

INDEX

Plain numbers (3) refer to the text and written sources. Italic numbers (3) refer to a picture.